LESSONS
ON
EXPULSION

LESSONS ON EXPULSION

poems

Erika L. Sánchez

GRAYWOLF PRESS

This publication is made possible, in part, by the voters of Minnesota through a Minnesota State Arts Board Operating Support grant, thanks to a legislative appropriation from the arts and cultural heritage fund, and a grant from the Wells Fargo Foundation. Significant support has also been provided by Target, the McKnight Foundation, the Amazon Literary Partnership, and other generous contributions from foundations, corporations, and individuals. To these organizations and individuals we offer our heartfelt thanks.

Published by Graywolf Press
250 Third Avenue North, Suite 600
Minneapolis, Minnesota 55401

www.graywolfpress.org

Published in the United States of America

ISBN 978-1-55597-778-8

2 4 6 8 9 7 5 3 1
First Graywolf Printing, 2017

Library of Congress Control Number: 2016951419

Cover design: Mary Austin Speaker

Cover art: Judithe Hernández, *The Purification*. www.judithehernandez.com

For my family:
Cata, Gus, Omar, Nora, Mario, Matteo, and Sofia

Contents

Love's an immigrant, it shows itself in its work.
It works for almost nothing.

—*Larry Levis*

LESSONS
ON
EXPULSION

Quinceañera

Summer boredom flutters its
sticky wings. You guzzle
cooking wine, gag on the old whiskey
you find in the pantry.
In the warmth of your bedroom,
you pierce your navel
with a safety pin, slice
the skin you hide beneath
your billowy dresses. Glitter-eyed
in the murky dance clubs,
you snort blow until the dregs
trickle down your throat and
shock your sluggish heart.
You dance in the frenetic
lights, the *untz untz* vibrating
your face and skull until
morning. But everywhere,
the pain suckles you. Everywhere,
you hold its lumpy head to your breast
like a saint. A fat man in a basement
tattoos a scraggly moon
on your hip, anything to smother
the soft and constant vertigo, to stitch
a spirit so riddled with leeches.
Some evenings you brim
with the sky's quiet bruising—
colors as beautiful as the spilled
brains of a bird. Such a fucked
holiness, you think. Weeping,
you read Walt Whitman—*the blow,*
the quick loud word,
the tight bargain, the crafty
lure. You hold a mirror to study
your tender socket. *May we eat*

and drink in remembrance
of the body. Oh, how the salt sings.
One morning you cut your hair
slowly then shear it altogether.
Whether that which appears
so is so, or is it all flashes
and specks? In that slurry
of August, the silence climbs you
like a man until you hear
the meaty flaps of God inside you.

Spring

On the bus to Granada,
you touch me in the afternoon sun,
and say my breasts
feel like ripe peaches,
that the rows of twisted trees
are olive groves, that it's been so long
since you've seen mountains.

I undress in the musty hostel
and suck on sour oranges
on the unmade bed.

I hear your lit cigarette
all the way from the bathroom.
You return smelling sharp like soap,
setting my nipples aflame.

The night you left was hot,
and I sweated, swathed in yellowed
sheets, trying to convince myself
that the world was still
beautiful without you.

These moments are burnt milk.
They're lucid semen trailing
down a crisp, white sheet.
Sometimes I think I'd break
glass with them if I could.

Sometimes when I am alone like this,
I think I hear your mouth, your stupid mouth
agape—the wet earth of my desire.

And I want to hook my fingers in you:
a hunger still unraveling
like silk in the stomach.

Narco

Highway of Death—the indifference
of snakes. Sky is ripe and everywhere
the colors are breaking. *¿Quién es el jefe*
más jefe? In the filmy stillness, Possum-face
carries a bucket of heads and spills them
like marbles. *La yerba, el polvo, las piedras—*
Que traguen fierro los cabrones,
¡yo soy el más chingón de Pisaflores!
Rompe-madres, gazing at mountains
the color of elephant skin, pulls a woman
from a bus and onto the thorns and dirt:
White hiss of heat. Hummingbirds. Milkweed.
A pack of spotted horses turn to the foaming
moon. *May God bless you all and lead you*
toward righteousness. Under the final gash
of light, Rompe-madres wipes the sweat
from his eyes, and ties her panties to a creosote bush—
a colony of vultures waiting for its tribute.

La Cueva

The glittering women swing
their hips like eternal bells. With pink,
histrionic mouths they sing: *Who is this*
in the mirror? Why won't you love me?
Why won't you let me be?
The costumes are small eruptions,
fabrics twisted and impossibly stitched—
a geisha bride, a cowgirl princess.
Beneath the unforgiving lights, the synthetic
yellow wigs startle the brown
clay of skin. Briefly, we see
how they've learned to wipe the smeared
mirrors inside them. The men
with the factory hands raise their fingers
to the hormone-softened
faces—a love flimsy as a wet yellow
dress. In the darkness, the matronly breasts
hang low and exhausted, though there won't be
children to nurse from them. *The body*
is not a hieroglyph but a triumph.
In the morning, the men will rise
for mass. With their wives they'll sing
¡El Señor resucitó! And as they clap
their hands alleluia, the smell, that singular
funk that springs from the body,
will weep from their callused palms.

Amá

In *One Hundred Years of Solitude*,
Márquez wrote that we are birthed
by our mothers only once, but life obligates
us to give birth
to ourselves over and over.

I'm sorry, Amá.
I know you think only white people leave
their families.
I undid my braids too early, I know.
It started when the blood
began to flow,
as if something inside me
kept unraveling.

I packed my bags one night
and left without a word.
Left like a gypsy, you said.

On my way to Tehuantepec,
I think about my own birth—
my head peeking out
from my own vagina.

In my hand I hold a bird
of paradise
that I bought from a boy
at a crossing.

Amá, I think of you
as I watch mountains,
women who carry
baskets on their heads,
dresses stitched
with jungle patterns.

Amá, I leave because
I feel like an unfinished
poem, because I'm always trying
to bridge the difference.

Amá, I wanted to tell you
about the parade in Oaxaca
that saved me.

About how I looked for your God
then mine in the desert,
about the pomegranate I shared
with a woman on the street
whose face was brown and creased
like yours.

Letter from New York

Every street—fried meat and onion,
smears of shit and a gaggle
of gadgets. What is the soul
but this endless circuitry,
the bright and pitiful idea
you carry of yourself?
Everything *open open*.
When you say available,
what you mean is pornographic.
Like a muted orgasm,
you are wet and brimming
with vague disgust.
In the subway station, a man picks
his skin and examines it—
feeling generous, he tells you
he'd like to share his findings.
Rat song, rat baby, rat cloud
in the heavens above. The rich smell
of baked garbage and coconut curry.
Fifth Avenue: a woman's cupped hands
catch her dog's excrement
as the dignified ferrets talk numbers.
Tiny mouths moist with want.
This is their desire: to slice
dollar bills and sauté them
in fragrant oil. Greed is Saturn
swallowing his own son, a man erect
with both fear and hunger.
The woman in fishnet panties strokes
the fruit in a street cart, musk
of hangover so warm and thick
you'll carry it inside your mouth for days.
The sound of wet brooms.
Listen: froth, water, concrete,

the absence and sputter of evening.
Tomorrow and tomorrow and tomorrow—
In your flamboyant despair,
you fail to suck the sweetness
from all that is good and holy.
Watch the pigeons so lovely
in their suffering! In the melted fat
of the hour, a crust-punk chokes
his dog in an empty park.
I'm sorry, I'm sorry, I'm sorry,
the dog whimpers, licking the filth
from his wounded feet.

Self-Portrait

In the white cream
of my lie,

I swallow warm pennies,

listen to the church bells
in the distance—

So much depends
upon insertion.

Just look at all this
face hunger!

Even my peaches
are obscene.

Don't you hear my name
dissolve like the body

of Christ?

*Siempre salgo
con el Jesús en la boca.*

Always tearing
at the hollyhocks,

always so slick
with summer.

Under the corpulent
clouds,

I feed the birds
of my failures,

so tenderly!

My tongue grows plump
as a greedy slug.

Again and again,
an umbrella

opens inside me.

Orifice of heaven—
the twilight comes

like a soiled miracle,

bright as my own
awful pink,

and how like a fever
it dazzles.

Las Pulgas

Santiago Meza López, known as "el Pozolero"
in the Mexican news media, has confessed to
dissolving the remains of 300 people in acid while
working for a top drug trafficker.

—The New York Times *(January 24, 2009)*

Even the trees here cringe—a heat
sticky like tamarind pulp.

The blindfolded bull is alone again,

walks in dusty circles around the block
and tries to lift the cloth
by blowing through his nose.

> *Juárez: behind the Hollywood Club*
> *(Live Girls XXX),*
>
> *an elegant skeleton*
> *on the back of his silk shirt.*
>
> *A necklace of dried nipples*
> *lies on his chest.*
>
> *He lowers his head: eyelids*
> *tattooed with open eyes.*
>
> *In the name of the holy . . .*

The town is named after fleas,
where the narcotraffickers have built

palaces bordered by concrete walls
embedded with broken cola bottles.

Next door, Jovita washes shit
from the tripe. In the river, she scrubs
until it's bright as teeth,

until no excrement
remains in the honeycomb pattern.

Jovita's son, the boy nicknamed Mal Hecho—
badly made—runs along the river

chasing chickens, huaraches slapping
against his cracked feet.

He knocks at every house,
collects slop

to feed the pigs. When he's finished,
he climbs a ladder
to peer next door, careful

not to touch the broken glass.
He studies the macaws

spreading their wings and snickers
when they squawk *¡cabrón! ¡cabrón!*

> *In a Tijuana club, a young woman straddles*
> *a man. He tugs her neon panties,*
>
> *and she is not shaved but he doesn't care. Black*
> *lights flicker, illuminate his teeth,*
>
> *the acne pits on his cheeks. Everyone moving*
> *in slow motion, like an old filmstrip,*
>
> *like what is happening*

couldn't possibly be true. There are mirrors
at every angle, everyone multiplied

by 6, 8, 10

impossible to know
whose body belongs to whom.

The woman turns around—

Mal Hecho and other boys gather
in a burnt-yellow house

at the edge of town where they watch Lucha Libre

on a scrambled screen and cheer
as they steady the hanger antenna.

The walls are covered in newspaper—
headlines like "Turismo Zapatista" and

"El 'Pozolero' pide disculpas."

    First, ass in face, then she lowers herself,
       lets him trace the spidery angel

    wings faded to green
       on her back. He drags his tongue
    along his teeth and remembers

    how easily a body
       dissolves in a vat
    of acid, how first, the flesh
    breaks away,
       how only the bones endure.

The Loop

The silences are copulating again. Look,
a woman so hungry her insides eat her other insides. ← signifying pregnancy
What are you crying about now? See, a black hole
of a mouth: *eat, eat, eat.* The cupcakes
are porno pink and they make you feel sexy!
It's the everyday accretion
of desire—the American
glory hole. A boss-man yelping and yelping
in a corner. Who are the office harpies
and who are the buzzards? (So many
mouth-breathers!) Beelzebub flaps Satan
his frozen wings and it's getting chilly in here.
What has the television taught the girls to say?
With their lips all plumped with hot goo.
Pixel this. Pixel that. Pixel your ugly face!
Your silence is a sealed jar of water,
little pariah. Outside, men and women Social outcast
carry pictures of dead fetuses.
The children hold them, too.
Every day, you say, *I am a person, I am a person.* ← said by fetus
It's winter and your feet are wet
again. You wave hello to the friendly rats.
Why do you flounder so easily in holes?
Do you suffer from cholera of the brain?
Check *yes* or *no.* The day goes on picking ⎫ I see this as the day
the meat from its teeth. ⎭ moving on w/o thinking
about her experiences

Could pair w/ Hija de la Chengada

17

Lavapiés

Madrid, Spain

Ripe fruit in my hands at the market. The sharp smell of ginger. I wait six months for him to visit me here, like a body on the verge of fever. My tiny kitchen that week—pots hissing, smoke swirling. The January air slips in from an open window. Broken cinnamon sticks. Frost. After dinner we crush the moist hash, mix it with cheap tobacco, and roll it in rice paper. When we are heavy with lentils and smoke, we braid our bodies together on my twin bed. I dig my face into his beard. The neighbors are yelling in Arabic, and I can't sleep when he is next to me. For breakfast, we eat two slippery eggs and drink coffee with frothy cream. At noon we finally manage to unhook ourselves and leave my apartment. It's Sunday and the streets of Lavapiés are fresh with dog shit, and the bohemians with ragged hair are playing guitar on the corner of Valencia and Miguel Servet. Women wrapped in orange saris are bargaining for vegetables. As we pass the rotisserie chickens in a café window, the three-legged dog follows us, begs us for food. That night on the train to the airport, I watch an ugly baby being breastfed by its gorgeous mother. He nudges me, says to stop staring, *stop being rude.* I tell him that I'm thinking about his wife, and he asks me if I could stand it and I say yes. At night when he is gone, I massage cocoa butter onto my nipples, rub my shaved legs on clean sheets, hold my fingers in my mouth until I fall asleep. Today I stand in a grocery store digging my nails into a ginger root. Smelling it like a goddamn fool.

Portrait of a Wetback

You cross the viridian scum
of river—
           wispy-tongued. The sun

whisking your deepest marrow.

A walk to the horizon
                with the bleakness
        on your shoulders:

     Mictlán,
                place of the fleshless,
electric-wired fences.

     Helicopters circle and circle
above you like buzzards.

     The desert thirst?
                A lit branch
in your throat.

       Jaguar, devourer
       of the sun.

You want to preserve this

in a jar of vinegar: the bright skull
        of the moon,

     the cloud white as a mistake.

When the guttural
              desert song begins,

when the bats descend,

      Xolotl, dog-headed man, god
of fire,

      drags you through the ragged

hole of a wire fence.

      Look, the gods wait for you

on their haunches.

The lights flash white
          and the sirens begin

as your brittle gaze
              still skins the beauty

from this paradise.

Lessons on Expulsion

I discipline my waist
and lean

against the heated coconut.

The day is gray as a face,
and my sin

clear as the hoofmarks
in the carmine.

What is God to me

but an open-mouthed
stranger?

I stepped across a viper
and still

the forked tongue
flickers in my hollow.

You see, my lust

will never
know death nor harvest:

elixir of hellebore, colocynth
salt, stick,

and mouse shit.

I run in circles
and bathe in the hateful river.

This grain, this
wild greedy thing

he's left me plumping

so paltry
and mulish.

Mercury, mandrake—

I am only a girl

with this brilliant black
nest of eagerness.

Over and over, my mother
calls to me,

my name

a reckless ribbon
in the gloaming.

When the clouds part
like stupid lovers,

I close my eyes and press
myself against

the eucalyptus tree.

I let the leeches
crawl until nightfall.

Hija de la Chingada

1.

The men whistle from their trucks
though you're only 13 and your breasts

are still tucked
meekly inside you.

Every day after school, the factory men yell
mamacita,

make noises like sucking
mangoes.

Technically, you could be a little mother—

But what do you know of sex?
You with the flapping

T-shirts and glasses the size of platters.

2.

One evening you come home
an hour late

and your mother calls you

hija de la chingada. ←— whore, basically

*Te pregunta ¿en dónde estás
abriendo las patas?*

What boy have you been fucking?

Your ghost-father
sits on the couch cracking peanuts

watching a Mexican gameshow—bugles and maracas,

and big-titted women dancing
with a geriatric host.

3.
Finally, when your plump little body
wants what it wants,

when you are bent in the arc
of desire,

you take a man
inside your mouth

in beautiful gulps
of summer,

until the shame clicks
its way toward you
like an ancient insect.

How many times will the rapid pumps
leave you heaving

in the bathroom?

4.

When your mother finds a condom in your pocket,
she slaps your mouth with the intention

of breaking your teeth.

She tells you this.

Birth control? *Aspirina*, she says.
You put the aspirin between your knees
and hold it tight.

5.

Now you say you're a grown woman
who can fuck her way across the world,
if she wants.

But when you wrap yourself
around your man,
when he yanks your hair
the way you like,

you still ask him to pretend
as if you hold a beautiful rapture
between your legs.

You still ask him to pretend
as if you're human.

On the Eve of the Tepehuán Revolt

November 1616

They are so wretched—these sons of dogs

> have nothing
> with which to pay tribute.

Tepehuán, Acaxee, Xixime. ← Mexican tribes

> A naked man under a cypress
> skins a coyote.

O, Father, forgive us
our daily terrors—

> What creatures are we

> thanking and thanking
> the gobs of darkness?

epademic – 80% indiginous pop. died

Rabid with cocoliztli—

> I ask pardon
> for those who do not adore thee.

> Even those who suckled

> upon your language

> still howl to stars
> when they shake with pestilence.

Every night I dream of scissors—

> *cría cuervos y te sacarán los ojos.*
> if you raise crows, they'll peck out your eyes

On this feast of the Blessed Virgin,

> I watch a band of gaunt horses

gather in a hushed circle—silence

so tentacled, so deep

it grows its own silence.

Guerra a fuego y sangre: when the bones clatter
a war of fire + blood
from the sapodilla trees,

when the rope-suckers pray

beneath the angry smear
of morning

my love comes slithering—
What is life but a cross

over rotten water?

Speaker

· Evropean
· maybe a priest, a conquistador?

To You on My Birthday

Face it, our tired metaphors loomed over us—
the dead blowfish in Puerto Vallarta, the white owl
perched atop the church in Oaxaca, the typhoid
in the Caribbean. But we are here again, the ocean.
The waves taking my breath like that
nocturnal cactus flower last night. You didn't
notice me prick my fingers
on its spindly silver needles,
you couldn't even smell the jasmine.

We hide away in the hotel—*La Hacienda de Cortés*.
A toilet full of red ants, fly strips flapping in the breeze,
a broken flower pot on the dresser.
You lie next to me—husk of spirit, bituminous
and evasive. Your words spilling like froth as white
collects in the creases of your lips. I turn
my back to you, then suddenly, silence.

A man is selling oysters
outside—*¡Ostiones! ¡Ostiones!*
A baby is crying. You touch me first,
then our bodies crack
together on the faded flowered sheets,
the sand making its way up,
way up in me.

We are tangled here now,
you taciturn and contemplative,
me tracing the arabesques of the curtains
with my eyes, the particles swirling
and dipping in the sunlight.

This is ridiculous, I think,
then suddenly I remember us
at the Chinese pizza place in the Dominican Republic:
the whining fluorescent light, the greasy
and brackish pizza, and the Chinese man
taking our order in English with that Dominican lilt.
I laugh and you don't ask me why.

Later, I drop the four bottles of Coronas; they shatter
all over the floor, so you carry me
to the bed, pick the flakes of glass
carefully from my feet, and say you don't
love me anymore. You had said it before,
but you say it again.

Now here we are,
all wrong, the ocean hissing
outside and us lying here sweating and nauseated.
The smell of frying cod.

I open the curtains, draw the hair
from my eyes, and watch
a clumsy yellow boat
waddling away from the dock.

Mexico, the ocean—where we began
when we were young and where we end,
almost equally young.

But that must be worth something, right?
Beauty is all about symmetry, isn't it?

Baptism

When the soft mouth of a word unhinges,
it is sticky, it is feral. Beneath the plum tree
I've woven my gray hair into a blanket.
Do you think I'm pretty crouched like this?
See, I am my own whore. Watch me
swallow my own fingers. My head a wild tangle
full of creatures. Do you hear that—the lovely hooves
and mangled pianos? The egg I hold inside my chest,
it's what the darkness ate. In the hot swamp,
in the battering sunlight, I tie my braid
around my neck and bury my name
until it's silent as a jewel. Feel my salt
burn in the cracks of your lips, feel the fat
pulse of my tender throat.
It's the shudder of beauty. No,
no, the shutter. Watch me dance
on borders in this dirty dress,
until my wig catches fire.

Crossing

la golondrina que de aquí se va
o si en el viento se hallará extraviada
buscando abrigo y no lo encontrará

—*Pedro Infante*

My parents leave the land blooming
with dust, locusts, their long hair
trailing behind them, into the wet flesh
ocher of the desert—ghost flowers,
Spanish needles. North.

> *Right there—across the river*
> *there are all kinds*
> *of magical instruments,*
> *and we keep on living here like donkeys.*

And we keep treading on the wires.

They move through turbid water, air
thick with mosquitoes. Sometimes coyotes
are not desert wolves, they're men
with mustaches, mirrored
sunglasses, who shove my shivering
parents into the trunk of a Cadillac,
who study my mother's wet-startled body.

In Chicago, we live in basements—the rattle
of heaters, jaundiced paint.
The smell of beans boiling, breaking
their skins. Everything fried up
in pig grease.

Crossing
. the border
. the atlantic — USA → Spain
. Columbous
. sign of the cross (crossing oneself)

The roaches make nests in our toys.
One makes its way inside my shoe
and comes out in school.
Another crawls
inside my brother's ear to start a home
until my mother drowns it
out with alcohol.

I exist because you see me.

You will not work like us. You will not work like a donkey,

my mother says
in factory heat, the murmur
of machines.

My meek brother inside his bedroom reading
The Grapes of Wrath, The Communist Manifesto, The Catcher in the Rye.
He is a good son.

Meanwhile, I carve my body
with pre-Columbian numbers, dye my hair
indigo, crimson,
plot rebellion.

self harm
→ Identifies more as indigenous than European.

I say *conscience* when I mean *conscious.*
To the doctor I describe the pain as existential tumors.
I say that the cuts are bloodletting.

I cross the Atlantic
like no one in my family ever has,
to live among the civilized,
drink wine, and read Cervantes.
Back to the motherland, some tell me.

But this is not my mother.
This looks nothing like my mother.

When asked where I am from,
what can I possibly say?
I am you, in part, I suppose,
I want to say, but I don't.

487 years ago
people here crossed the ocean
and savagely fused with the inhabitants.
467 years later
my parents crossed the border
in the trunk of a Cadillac.
I was born in Chicago.

her parents crossed the boorder

I dance in the foreign streets,
devour oysters until I feel guilty,
light candles, and believe in God.

I smoke until my mouth hurts.

While I'm at the Prado enjoying Goya and Velázquez,
my father is rising before the sun
to assemble air filters.

On my way home
I want to read a poem aloud on the Metro
about my illiterate grandmother, about my father
with the glue burns on his hands.

guilty conscience

Sometimes between sleep and waking life
I think I'm in another city.
The mornings taste like bruises.

I call my mother to explain
how I scour landscapes, fold them
and keep them in a soft leather bag.

I tell her how I want to understand
the violence tangled in this tissue,
the desert threaded in this flesh.

Saudade

In the republic of flowers I studied
the secrets of hanging clothes I didn't
know if it was raining or someone
was frying eggs I held the skulls
of words that mean nothing you left
between the hour of the ox and the hour
of the rat I heard the sound of two
braids I watched it rain through
a mirror am I asking to be spared
or am I asking to be spread your body
smelled like cathedrals and I kept
your photo in a bottle of mezcal
semen-salt wolf's teeth you should have
touched my eyes until they blistered
kissed the skin of my instep for thousands
of years sealed honey never spoils
won't crystallize I saw myself snapping
a swan's neck I needed to air out
my eyes the droplets on a spiderweb
and the grace they held who gave me
permission to be this person to drag
my misfortune on this leash made of gold

Orchid

In Cicero the white prostitutes
in front of the Cove Motel lean into cars—
knotted hair, limp breasts
jiggling under their tattered T-shirts.

We are seven when we watch from our steps
sucking on tamarind candy, confused.
Aren't blonde women supposed to be beautiful?
Then I am 22 in Musée d'Orsay and finally

standing before Manet's *Olympia*. Her square face
and taut body, stiff hand over her sex. A woman
who can slight the black servant, snub the flowers.
She waits for a milk-faced man who will suck her

open like an oyster, make feverish love to her, crumple
the orchid behind her ear. Next, red light
district, Amsterdam: women in glass boxes:
backs impossibly arched, full breasts

spilling out of shiny lingerie. I wonder
how the old ones with missing teeth
compete with them. Behind
a cracked door, a woman rinses

her mouth and spits into a sink.
On Calle Montera, Madrid—the center of the city
near the exact center of the country—women
from Africa, Latin America, and dissolved

European countries are in front of McDonald's,
pulling on sleeves and listing prices. A teenage boy wants
to know if they offer student discounts. A graying man
approaches a black transvestite with golden hair

and asks, how much to have sex with the dog?
In Bilbao, I watch a news exposé in a fusty hostel
we've named Kafka. A Russian woman
named Katya has been sold in Istanbul for $1,000,

then forced to live in a brothel where men insert
bizarre objects, perform acts from Marquis de Sade
pencil sketches. Katya cries and her tears slice
through thick slabs of orange makeup.

My boyfriend lives next to a motel now,
in the urban blight of a desert city,
and after lunch today, a woman in gray sweats
walks past his house toward a mammoth SUV.

She walks slowly, as if splintered, as if
something is already inside her.

The Poet at Fifteen

after Larry Levis

You wear faded black
and paint your face white as the blessed
teeth of Jesus
because brown isn't high art
unless you are a beautiful savage.

All the useless tautologies—

This is me. I am this. I am me.

In your ragged
Salvation Army sweaters, in your brilliant

awkwardness. White dresses
like Emily Dickinson.

I dreaded that first Robin,
so, at fifteen you slash
your wrists.

You're not allowed
to shave your legs in the hospital.

The atmosphere
that year: sometimes you exist
and sometimes you think you're Mrs. Dalloway.

This is bold—existing.

You do not understand your parents
who understand you less:
your father who listens to ABBA after work,
your mother who eats expired food.

How do you explain what you have done?
With your hybrid mouth, a split tongue.

How do you explain the warmth
sucking you open, leaving you
like a gutted machine?

It is a luxury to tell a story.

How do you explain
that the words are made by more
than your wanting?

Te chingas o te jodes.

At times when you speak Spanish, your tongue
is flaccid inside your rotten mouth:

desgraciada, sin vergüenza.

At the hospital they're calling your name
with an accent on the *E*. They bring you
tacos, a tiny golden crucifix.

Your father has run
all the way from the factory.

Kindness

Estelí, Nicaragua

The barefoot boys are little men,
sticky children wielding machetes,
slicing weeds.

Dogs in gaunt elegance
bow their heads and follow—

scabs and bubble gum on their matted fur.

We say if there were ever animals
to kill themselves, it would be these dogs.

The girls we never see. I imagine
they are grinding corn
or rubbing their hands raw
on soap and slabs of concrete
in the morning fog.

⊚ ⊚ ⊚

In my dream last night,
I was pregnant and didn't want it,
so I used nails.

That's all I remember: nails
and a birth not celebrated.

⊚ ⊚ ⊚

How easily we protest
discomfort: the heat making nests
in the thickets of our bodies, the insects
like scissors on our ankles, the shit
and static water.

How we learn to praise
a grain of rice
when we hear the slight gurgle
of hunger in the flute of the body.

How we learn to love
an egg.

We can eat until we are shamefaced and swollen
with happiness and light and the neverending.

           ◎ ◎ ◎

What can milk say?
Victorious milk,
milk like mucous
in your throat—a pearl.
Cruel milk with a hair in it.

The kindness of milk.

           ◎ ◎ ◎

Granada: a British man with bleached hair
walks barefoot in the street
in his imagined bohemia, over glass
scattered like confetti.

Two backpackers
with sores like tropical flowers,
        lustrous sores,
sores like opal.

A young boy kisses his fingers
and presses them to our cab window.

⊚ ⊚ ⊚

In Estelí, the rattle
of history, a photograph—

Miliciana de Waswalito: Matagalpa, Nicaragua.

A radiant Sandinista breastfeeding,
a rifle on her back.

⊚ ⊚ ⊚

In the morning my period comes
like a hot and languid Sunday afternoon.

My breasts still remembering
the milk the body can brew.

Kingdom of Debt

According to a 2015 report from the University of San Diego's Justice in Mexico project, 138,000 people have been murdered in Mexico since 2006.

They call it the corner of heaven: *[handwritten: talking about drug Cartels]*
a laboratory, a foot at the throat
of an empire. Before the holy
dirt, the woman with the feline gait
waits with tangled hair, mouth
agape—the letter X marked
on what's left of her breasts
and face. *Nuestra Belleza
Mexicana.* A roped mule
watches a man place a crown
on her severed head. Tomorrow
the queen will be picked clean
by the kindness of the sea.
Shuttered shops and empty
restaurants. Stray dogs couple
in a courtyard. Under a swaying
palm tree, a cluster of men
finger golden pistols, whisper,
aquí ni se paran las moscas. *[handwritten: not even flies will stop here]*
Two boys, transfixed, watch
a pixelated video: a family fed
to a swarm of insatiable pigs.
A butcher sweeps blood
from an empty street. *Death
is my godmother*, he repeats.
Death is a burnt mirror.
When the crackling stereo
dithers between stations—*amor*

de mis amores, sangre de mi alma—
a gaggle of silent children
gather before a sputtering
trash bin. Together they watch
the terror hover like flies.

Love Story

In a field of broken antlers,
I'm holy

as the grass
where a deer has slept.

And still, this is the hell
we make together,

the pleasure
of tangled violins.

Each night I inhale
my own wings

when my skin
remembers asters.

Understand this: the pull
of my womb,

why we fuck in a field
of dandelions.

How loathsome is that?

A woman who cuts her name
into a cypress.

But the story always begins
with a lie, doesn't it?

A dark room full of birds

where I slapped the bread
from your hands

and drowned
in a bowl of water.

So much magical thinking
in that swallow

of summer the women
in my dreams

never came with their mouths
open.

Blame my salted brain,
or the fever tree that fingers

the sky with questions.

Listen—

you can hear my heart beat
with the humiliation.

A Woman Runs on the First Day of Spring

—Chicago

When I am a stranger to my own
ruin, twilight reminds me
to give alms to my best sins.
March: the city is purging
in the humility of worms, salt
washing from the grasses.
When I breathe in, I say thank you.
When I breathe out, I say gone,
I say garden, I say guns.
Three crows devour the dead
rat. *Look at all that booty*,
the man mutters and blows
me kisses. The sky is worthless
and my bulbous ass is always
a dinner bell. I run farther,
I run with a feather inside
my ear, I run from a bird
with a broken neck and follow
the sound of thawing snow.
Aren't we all boundless
though? The way a dream
secretes the morning after,
the way moths feed on the eyes
of fawn. Two and not two—
vines that strangle trees never
say they're sorry. I reach
the lake with this grateful
ache in my throat. And if I say
my body is its own crumbling
country, if I say I am always
my own home—then
what does that make me?

Girl

In the evening hum of traffic
and cicadas, you watch
the ugly curtains flutter
in hot wind: Little Orphan
Annie and her ridiculous flame
of hair. Outside two sparrows
bathe in dust, a man thrusts
against a prostitute who gasps
when she sees you in the window—
always the little spectator,
feral and plugged with squalor.
Finally, you've learned to crawl
inside the meat of your silence.
On the way home from school,
you study the factory's chemical
blooms in the distance. A man
with a tumor glowing on his head
exits the rank motel on the corner.
You crash your bike into a boy
by mistake, and his porcine father
screams at you until he's hoarse:
Fuck you, you motherfucking bitch!
Shaking, you run inside,
and for months you're convinced
he'll find a way to kill you.
Weed lot in the muted
sunset: the retarded boy pulls
down his pants and a circle
of kids laugh at his stiff, red penis.
It looks like an alien, you whisper
to your friend. The women
with black eyes and wizened faces
call you *honey*, call you *sweetie*.
A man on the street tears the gold

necklace from your mother's neck—
this is how you learn that nothing
will belong to you. In your mangled
language, you'll count all the reasons
you wish to die, the apartment bristling
with roaches. Always the smell
of corn oil. But what right do you have
to complain about anything,
with your clean socks and fat
little stomach? Burnt pies from
the thrift bakery you shove down
your desperate gullet. What can
you blame but your rootless
eye? Your mind so soft and full
of hysterical light. You've already
learned that your body is a lie.

Juárez

Behind The Great Wall of Mexico,
pork fat crackles
and crackles. Bright pink

corpses lie coiled in nipple cacti,
Apache plumes.

Beyond the green, green

lawns and the burnt
smell of plastic.

Beyond the Pemex—
gasoline rainbows iridescent
as peacock feathers.

A ribbon flutters in a cottonwood.

     The body as eruption.
     The body as contraband.

An empty river runs and runs.

         ◎ ◎ ◎

Dirt and thistle
wait for Tlaloc and his water jugs

while the maquilas flower
like tumors on a spine.

Somewhere, a man serves
champagne, a pair of breasts
on a plate.

Another leaves the openness
of the desert in a pickup.

His bumper sticker reads: *Todo es posible
con Cristo.*

¡Viva Cristo, El Rey!

⊙   ⊙   ⊙

On the news they describe the victims
as young, slim,
and dark-complexioned,

poor daughters of the working class.

After my shower today, I'm startled
by my own nakedness.

⊙   ⊙   ⊙

No ocean to drown:

wet concrete, sand, locusts.

An ethereal hand
fingering dust.

A hunger, a name, an agreement.

⊙   ⊙   ⊙

In my dream last night—
thousands of pink crosses.
Lightning streaked the violet
sky, and on my knees,

I scratched every name, peeled
each letter with my nails,
buried them in mud and ash.

⊚   ⊚   ⊚

A dark woman's small hands
assemble circuitry.

She breathes plastic, glue,
memorizes the music
of machines.

For $5.40 a day,
her nose will not stop bleeding.

On her way home—summer
is flaming in the horizon.

She picks a flower
the color of a perfectly painted mouth.

Self-Portrait

Holding a suitcase full of feathers, I scan a woman
with a barcode on her neck—my god
is a filth-eater. Tomorrow suckles
my left breast   and the bitch
just won't stop talking. Call me she
of the two faces. Call me she who gobbles
sin.   My silence is an animal
dressed in hooks. My body   is a gift
like a bowl of coins.   Hear me break
the delicate bones of spring.   I scrape
my teeth   against the tree bark.
I can't stop inseminating   myself.
I'm sorry. I apologize. Excuse me. I beg
for forgiveness.   Under the torched
gown of sky, you ride me   like a donkey.
And I let you.   My screams are nothing
but windows painted shut.   In the soft hole
of summer,   look how the world makes us
all supplicants.   Look how I die wringing
my hands   in light.

Forty-Three

The moment before death the air—
inexplicably—tastes of wet horse.
The chest expands and something
unspools like wet vines. In this land
of child-brides and teenage assassins,
a bus full of students dissolves
into the mountain mist. A retinue
of beheaded journalists mouth
clues while the young president
delivers platitudes. But what
do they matter? The students
don't know the kilos of heroin
stored below them. A boy of 18,
eyes gray as bathwater, charts
a man's face under his black
mask. *Why even bother?* the boy
wonders. The night's only
witnesses—the stars, an ocelot,
a single strand of hair caught
in a barbed wire. Even the zopilotes
won't eat the glut of the unsayable.
The blood-birds hiss and grunt
while a man with pointed teeth
whistles a love song. Why waste
time with metaphors? The body
is kindling. The body is a plastic
bouquet shriveled at a crossing.
The trees bow and weep, but
everybody knows the rain revises
nothing, the charred bones belong
to no one. Beyond the verdant
mountain, a caravan of mothers

and fathers beg a cankered country
for the locus of cruelty. Farther,
a troop of camouflaged men burn
fields of red poppies—those lovely
flowers of happiness and squalor.

Vieques

In a Pentecostal church, weeping women play the tambourine. We watch them writhe and sing from the hotel balcony, the music faint against the rustle of palms, the incantation of night frogs: *co-qui co-qui*. O soul, why do you feel so ragged? Everywhere—a violent fecundity. I draw a sun on your sunburn. In the bioluminescent bay, we are light itself, a glow so blue, the jelly of you quivers and quivers. Mosquitoes feast on our softest parts. In the morning, the faithful speak tongues on the beach, their hands open to the nothingness of the horizon. A black horse defecates in the ocean while the green sunset strums the finest wires inside us. I hold this all like paper sewn together. A brief happiness as fierce as the wet muscles of a horse. At dinner we pick at the shiny fish skins. We drink the piss-rum. We use words like tongue flowers.

Poem of My Humiliations

After the salt feast, I watched a bird peck at another bird who was
    already dead.

What I know best is the color of sun through my own eyelids.

And like those jubilant saplings, I am always so breathless and
    ignorant.

I once fucked a man who was unspeakably ugly, and it wasn't even
    winter.

What I mean is that I bludgeoned the palm fronds to keep from
    sobbing.

What I mean is that I lit a kite on fire and didn't say I was sorry.

The gaze of the deer was nothing if not victorious.

I once loved a man who was married to a martyr.

No, he was married to a goat. No, he was married to a ladder. What's
    the difference?

I cried on a toilet in the middle of New York City. Four times in one
    day. I counted. I promise.

That time I was stunned by my own pudendum. The smell.

Then I became ashamed of my shame, etcetera, infinity until the end
    of time itself.

The vulgarity of the orchid in all of its hooded glory is showy but
    exquisite.

The first time I ever came the light was weak and carnivorous.

I covered my eyes and the night cleared its dumb throat.

I heard my mother wringing her hands the next morning.

Of course I put my underwear on backward, of course the elastic
    didn't work.

What I wanted most at that moment was a sandwich.

But I just nursed on this leather whip.

I just splattered my sheets with my sadness.

Circles

Love, remove your fingers
from between

my ribs.

It's true; I cup the grief

as if it were milk, as if it were the last of water
spilled.

Quiet, you whistle in my brain
like a balloon.

What religion is this? Boredom
in spring.

Look at me.

The burn you've left
on my arm: wet orchids.

Tomorrow, I will braid you
an awful necklace

made of hair.

And when the meaning is all gutted
from the day,

I will delight
in the sticky mess, in a swirl

so deep I forget myself.

Go on—
carve up your favorite parts.

Hyacinth

On the morning of Jacinta's
birth, the air smelled animal.
The blind rooster forever
confused by the mysteries of light.
After her final gasp of gratitude,
Alondra wiped the slime
from the baby's eyes and pierced
her ears with golden spikes.
Soon she'll learn to swallow
the cactus spines, she murmured.
As a girl, Jacinta spooned
beans and swept dirt floors
with sodden brooms. Her father,
merchant of pigs, always speckled
the flimsy horizon. Alondra
grew inward: a bundle of rags
and sticks in a corner, a cocoon
of debris. On the rickety walls—
ashen saints with their eyes
rolled back in blessedness,
whites the color of old wedding
dresses. The scent of lard, cornhusks,
and illness. When the news
of her father's shame came
on horseback, Jacinta covered
her head with frayed linen
and beat his bloody clothes
against the river-rocks. What
does it mean to forgive?
For years she slapped her own
face in the faded mirrors.
Once, a man strummed
his broken guitar in the plaza
as a hunchback whistled

against a willow tree. It was there
that Severo's gaze finally
found her, covered her skin
like tar. Under a clipped moon,
his voice made one circle
and then another, until Jacinta
signed her name with the letter X
on a wet and frigid morning.
The poverty of love. Beads
of blood. The children came
like swarms of locusts: a constellation
of sores on a baby's face,
a womb marked by nothing.
In meager times, haughty
women bequeathed her
leftovers filled with napkins
and toothpicks—dregs from their
finest feasts. The bloody egg
was more than a bad omen,
they said. That night the wind
smelled like wet copper.
The diseased mare brayed
in the loud suck of mud,
and in her winged loneliness,
Jacinta severed her braids and begged
for the threat of miracles.

Capital

In the dream I sing to slums
and cathedrals

holding all of my worthless
shards of longing. (I told God

I was a bright silhouette
with her lips sewn shut.)

Arrastrada. I am a woman,
meek as a wet

cock. Watch how I shield
my ears from the tiny blades

of the cricket song,
but I still love

the way the evening rages on,
its endless shriek

of purple cloud. Even the killers
cross themselves

in the vespers' milky hush.

Listen, the chiclet boys whistle
for me in the distance,

a rusted trumpet plays itself
in a field of brambles.

With furred tongue, I watch
a woman float

in the glutted river.

Don't you see me? I bow to you,
glorious city,

city of love, city of atrophy,
where the body becomes a puzzle,

and the sky
is longer astonished.

Donkey Poem

Gentle beast, you carry Jesus
to Jerusalem.

And Jesus looks at the city

            and weeps for it.

     Equus asinus:

spine sucker
         thistle eater.

You lay unburied
under the Sierra Madre sun

         patas p'arriba—

      the vultures
already gorging
        on your stringy haunches.

     Burro humilde, burro sufrido

     bestia de la melancolía.

On a frozen mountainside,

     a peasant will dismount you and weep

as he tears into your vermilion

    meat.

Am not I thine ass,
upon which thou hast ridden
                              ever since I was thine

unto this day?

Erotic toiler.
Stubborn ungulate.

The ass
of every punchline.

          Every firstborn of a donkey
          you shall redeem

          with a lamb, or if you will not redeem it,
          you shall
                    break its neck.

5,000 years you plough
                    the cracked earth

and arrive with your crumbling
hooves.

        —A room full of howling

                    men whose eyes swell

with thirst and fever.

          Burro humilde, burro sufrido—

a dark and trembling woman

undresses
                    and kneels before you.

Six Months after Contemplating Suicide

Admit it—
you wanted the end

with a serpentine
greed. How to negotiate

that strangling
mist, the fibrous

whisper?

To cease to exist
and to die

are two different things entirely.

But you knew this,
didn't you?

Some days you knelt on coins
in those yellow hours.

You lit a flame

to your shadow
and ate

scorpions with your naked fingers.

So touched by the sadness of hair
in a dirty sink.

The malevolent smell
of soap.

When instead of swallowing a fistful
of white pills,

you decided to shower,

the palm trees
nodded in agreement,

a choir
of crickets singing

behind your swollen eyes.

The masked bird
turned to you

with a shred of paper hanging
from its beak.

At dusk,
hair wet and fragrant,

you cupped a goat's face

and kissed
his trembling horns.

The ghost?

It fell prostrate,
passed through you

like a swift
and generous storm.

Notes

"Quinceañera"

The lines "*the blow, / the quick loud word, / the tight bargain, the crafty / lure*" and "*Whether that which appears / so is so, or is it all flashes / and specks?*" were taken from Walt Whitman's "There Was a Child Went Forth."

"Crossing"

The lines "*right there—across the river / there are all kinds / of magical instruments, / and we keep on living here like donkeys*" were taken from *One Hundred Years of Solitude* by Gabriel García Márquez, translated by Gregory Rabassa.

"The Poet at Fifteen"

The line "*I dreaded that first Robin, so*" was taken from the opening of Emily Dickinson's poem (348).

Acknowledgments

Many thanks to the editors of the following magazines and journals, in which these poems were first published.

"Saudade," The Academy of American Poets *Poem-A-Day*
"Quinceañera" and "Poem of My Humiliations," *Boston Review*
"Portrait of a Wetback," *Copper Nickel*
"On the Eve of the Tepehuán Revolt" and "Donkey Poem," *diode*
"Kindness," *Drunken Boat*
"A Woman Runs on the First Day of Spring," ESPN.com
"Lessons on Expulsion," *Guernica*
"Self-Portrait (Holding a Suitcase)," *Gulf Coast*
"To You on My Birthday," "Amá," and "Spring," *Hanging Loose*
"Lavapiés," *Hayden's Ferry Review*
"Orchid" and "Las Pulgas," *Hunger Mountain*
"Quinceañera," "Donkey Poem," and "Portrait of a Wetback," National Public Radio
"Self-Portrait (In the White Cream)," *Nepantla*
"Hija de la Chingada," *Ostrich Review*
"Love Story," *The Paris Review*
"The Poet at Fifteen" (originally published as "Quinceañera") and "Vieques," *Pinwheel*
"Quinceañera," *Please Excuse This Poem: 100 New Poems for the Next Generation* (Viking, 2015)
"Circles," *Pleiades*
"Narco," "Kingdom of Debt," "Six Months after Contemplating Suicide," *Poetry*
"La Cueva," *The Southeast Review*
"Girl," "Letter from New York," and "Baptism," *Vinyl*
"Juárez," *Witness*

I am thankful for my mentors, friends, and family for providing such unwavering support as I wrote this collection over the past several years.

My appreciation for Jeff Shotts and the Graywolf family knows no bounds. Thank you for honoring my vision and helping me create the best version of this book. I couldn't have asked for a better publisher. Your belief in the power of poetry perpetually inspires me.

My deepest gratitude to Eduardo C. Corral, Rigoberto González, Dana Levin, Juan Felipe Herrera, and Eileen Myles for seeing the potential in my work and providing me with the encouragement to transcend myself. Your guidance means so much to me.

Thank you to Don Share, *Poetry*, and the Poetry Foundation for giving my poems a home and awarding me a 2015 Ruth Lilly and Dorothy Sargent Rosenberg Poetry Fellowship.

Thank you to the Unterberg Center at the 92nd Street Y for recognizing my work with a 2013 Discovery/*Boston Review* Poetry Prize.

Thank you to the Bread Loaf Writers' Conference for granting me a 2014 tuition scholarship.

I would like to acknowledge the Guild Complex for giving me the opportunity to attend *Kapittel*, the International Festival of Literature and Freedom of Speech in Stavanger, Norway, where I had the honor of meeting incredible exiled writers who bravely sacrificed their safety for the sake of art and justice.

Lynn Melnick and Brett Fletcher Lauer, I'm grateful to have been included in your anthology *Please Excuse This Poem: 100 New Poems for the Next Generation*, a beautiful, necessary, and transformative collection for young people.

To my CantoMundo family, I am blessed to have your love and community throughout my career.

Thanks to Phillip B. Williams, Kyle Churney, Steven Schroeder, and Dave Welch, who gave me invaluable feedback on my various drafts, and to my friends and peers for believing in me, even when I couldn't. This includes Adriana Díaz, Andrea Peterson, Elizabeth Schmuhl, Jacob Saenz, Jennifer Fitzgerald, Danielle Susi, Michael Harrington, Cristián Flores, Nayelly Barrios, Safiya Sinclair, Sara Brickman, Sara Inés Calderón, and countless others.

Shout out to the crew at Bridgeport Coffee House for cheerfully keeping me caffeinated this past year as I wrote and revised obsessively.

And lastly, to the Sánchez family, particularly my parents, who taught me how to cross borders, and all the women who came before me.

ERIKA L. SÁNCHEZ is the daughter of Mexican immigrants. She is a poet, essayist, and fiction writer, and the author of a young adult novel, *I Am Not Your Perfect Mexican Daughter* (Knopf Books for Young Readers, 2017). Her poetry has appeared in *Boston Review, Guernica,* the *Paris Review, Poetry,* and other publications, and her nonfiction has appeared in *Al Jazeera, Cosmopolitan,* ESPN.com, the *Guardian,* NBC News, *Rolling Stone, Salon,* and elsewhere. She has received a CantoMundo Fellowship, a Discovery/*Boston Review* Poetry Prize, a Fulbright Scholarship to Madrid, Spain, and a Ruth Lilly and Dorothy Sargent Rosenberg Poetry Fellowship from the Poetry Foundation. She is a 2017–2019 Princeton Arts Fellow.

The text of *Lessons on Expulsion* is set in Adobe Garamond Pro. Book design by Connie Kuhnz. Composition by Bookmobile Design and Digital Publisher Services, Minneapolis, Minnesota. Manufactured by Versa Press on acid-free, 30 percent postconsumer wastepaper.